NAVAJO: 1868-1968

NAVAJO: A CENTURY OF PROGRESS
was produced by K. C. Publications
in cooperation with the Navajo Tribe
as the first
in a continuing series commemorating
the Navajo Centennial

NAVAJO
A CENTURY OF PROGRESS
1868-1968

Edited by Martin A. Link

PUBLISHED BY THE NAVAJO TRIBE, WINDOW ROCK, ARIZONA

A LETTER FROM THE CHAIRMAN

The year, 1968, marks the 100th anniversary of the signing of the Treaty of Peace between the Navajo Tribe and the U. S. Government. This Treaty, signed by 29 Navajo headmen and ten officers of the U. S. Army on June 1, 1868, brought to an end a tragic period of suffering, hardship, deprivation and exile at the Bosque Redondo.

During the intervening century, the Navajo people have witnessed a substantial population increase and have undergone drastic and far-reaching changes in their economy, self-government, social status, education, and living conditions. However, in some areas, the Navajo people have only begun to solve some of the problems of poverty, land depletion, lack of modern utilities, and chronic unemployment. There is much work yet to be done. The Navajo people will pause often during this Centennial Year to honor their heritage, but throughout all these events, we will be preparing to make this the start of a bold new era of progress, growth, self-sufficiency, industrial and economic development for our deloved country.

Raymond Nakai, Chairman
Navajo Tribal Council

CONTENTS

Dineh: THE PEOPLE

From down in the Emergence Pit
  The Talking God moves with me
  up the black ladder
He moves with the rainbow
  To the edge of the Emergence pit
Blue-bird is humming before me
  Corn-Beetle is humming behind me
I, I am Sahanahray Bekayhozhon
  Before me all is beautiful
Behind me all is beautiful

In the beginning, our Hataatli Grandfathers tell us, there was darkness everywhere. And in that Underworld of Darkness, lived the Insect People, at peace with one another.

But after awhile, The People began to quarrel among themselves, and appealed to Tieholtsodi (Gatherer of waters) to settle their differences. He decreed that they leave the Land of Darkness, and this The People did, through a small hole in the eastern sky.

They came into the Second World, a world of blue and inhabited by the Swallow People. Soon, however, bitterness and jealousy spread between the newcomers and the Swallow People so once again The People climbed to the sky. To the south they found a passage and pushing through it, came upon the Third World, and its color was yellow.

The Third World was the land of the Grasshopper People and The People fared little better here than elsewhere. Soon they were again asked to leave, and with the help of the Holy Ones found an opening in the western sky and made their way to the Fourth World.

In this land of whiteness, The People prospered and lived in harmony with the birds and animals who dwelt there. But one day Coyote kidnapped the small daughter of Tieholtsodi, and out of revenge, he brought forth a great flood that covered the land. Through a large reed that sprang up miraculously, The People were able to escape the rising waters and emerge into this, the Present World.

With sacred earth brought up from the Underworld, The Holy Ones created four Mountains and adorned them with all the perfect forms of plants and animals, as well as Black Clouds, Male Rain and Immortality. To the East they prepared a mountain of White Shell and called it *Sisnajini* (Sierra Blanca Peak); to the South a mountain of Turquoise was named *Tso Dzil* (Mt Taylor); in the West a mountain of Abalone was called *Dook'o'osliid* (San Francisco Mountains); and to the North was placed a mountain made of jet and named *Dibentsaa* (Mount Hesperus). And all the lands contained therein were given to Earth People, the offspring of First Man and First Woman.

These People, Dineh, as we still call ourselves, spread out over the land and ranged from high mountain to parched mesa, from broad valley to deep canyon. Here was a country free and open, but also harsh and unrelenting. But it was our land and our forefathers challenged it with their strength, their patience, their adaptability, and their endurance.

They were an adventurous people; raiders and explorers. Their travels brought them into contact with other cultures, notably the Pueblo tribes along Rio Grande and the Utes and the Apaches. They learned and observed from their neighbors and intermarried so that their numbers would grow. Always they assimilated into our culture what they found good and useful and discarded what was not deemed important or helpful.

Here in the land between the four sacred mountains, our ancestors worked the land, prospered, and watched their families multiply. Faithfully were the prayer-songs and ceremonies conducted; ceremonies that were taught to them by the Yeis and Holy Ones, and the Dineh lived in dignity and harmony with all of creation.

From the Pueblo Indians, they learned the art of weaving and the techniques of cultivating corn, beans, squash and pumpkins. Our People soon became so skillful as farmers that the Tewa Indians called them "Navahoes" meaning "Cultivators of the Fields". Through the years, groups of Puebloans intermingled with the Dineh and originated such clans as the Naashashi, Tl'ogi, and Maii deeshgiizhnii.

Four hundred years ago a strange new race of man invaded this land of ours. Mounted on horses, their metal armor glittering in the sun, they came in search of precious metals and souls to save. One by one, the Pueblo strongholds fell before the Spanish onslaught, but the Navajo faded back into their canyons and watched from a distance. What they saw were animals that must truly be gifts from the Holy Ones. Sheep and cattle, they soon discovered, could provide food and clothing and the horse the mobility needed to hunt deer and raid their enemies.

By the 1700's, the People had taken up the life of stockraising, and, because the herds had to be constantly moved to new pastures, farming became less and less important. By this time too, the Navajo were keenly aware of the Spanish challenge to their ownership of the land. This land between the four sacred mountains was in jeopardy and the wrath of Navajo vengance was felt throughout the Southwest. Spanish-Mexican rancherias and villages were raided time and again by these fearless, swift warriors from the Dinehtah.

Soon after the United States declared war in 1846, on Mexico, it acquired the territories of New Mexico and Arizona. Now the Navajos faced a new enemy, but one more powerful and determined than the Spanish-Mexicans had been. After the Mexican War, settlers came, staked out their homesteads and plowed under the grass that was the life-blood of Navajo herds. In defiance of the Navajo a fort was built in our heartland, and for the next twenty years the land shuddered beneath the pounding hoofs of cavalry and warriors.

Finally, it was decided that the Navajos should no longer live on the land between the sacred mountains. Soldiers, under the command of Colonel "Kit" Carson, ravaged the country-side burning the fields of corn and destroying homes, orchards, and sheep. The People, starved into submission, surrendered in the winter and spring of 1864.

Nearly 7,000 Navajos made the trip of over 300 miles to the flat, wind-swept reservation situated on the banks of the Rio Pecos. It was a trip that would be forever remembered in sadness by our people. The terrible experience of being uprooted and expelled from our sacred homeland has left an indelible mark upon our heritage. The hardships endured, along with the tragedy, suffering and death which many of our people met, will be remembered by all as The Long Walk.

A TIME FOR SUFFERING

"I came searching for you;
*   you and I will begin our return, my grandchildren.*
We two are now leaving, my grandchild,"
*   Hashji-altye says to me.*
With the talking KEHTAHN in his right hand,
*   He encircles me with it, in a sunwise direction,*
*   and places it in my right hand;*
Encircling me, sunwise, with a rainbow,
*   he turns me, sunwise, towards himself;*
"We two will now start back, my grandchild,"
*   he says to me;*
"We two are now leaving, my grandchild,"
*   he says to me as I return to stand upon*
*   the rainbow.*

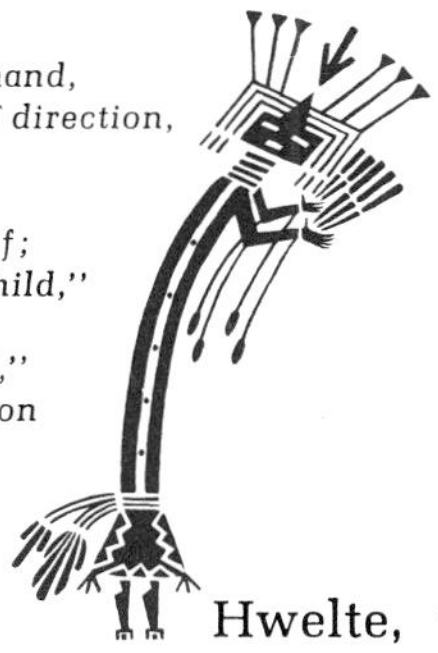

Hwelte, we called it, the Mexicans called it Bosque Redondo, and the American soldiers named it after the man who, twelve years earlier, had established Ft. Defiance — Colonel Edwin V. Sumner. But the place, regardless of the name was soon to symbolize death, hardship, suffering, inadequate food and lack of clothing. Nearly 2,000 of our people died of pneumonia and dysentery. Although they worked hard at it, attempts at developing farmlands were utter failures. In the spring of 1864, soon after their arrival, the Navajos cleared 3,000 acres for planting and constructed a series of irrigation canals from the Pecos River. However, shortly before harvest, a cut worm got into the corn crop and destroyed nearly all of it.

The corn, wheat and melon crops of 1865, expanded to 6,000 acres, were also a failure, with the corn again being devoured by the cut worms.

The following year the fields lay parched and dry under a blazing sun. The Pecos shriveled to a mere trickle as drought spread across the land. By this time, too, all available fire wood had been consumed and our people were making daily trips of nearly 25 miles to gather mesquite roots for fuel.

By 1867, the fields had become so impregnated with alkali that the corn grew only two feet high. The 7,000 Navajos still at Ft. Sumner by now were half-starved, diseased and terribly homesick. But at last their plight was seen by Washington. In May of 1868, several members of the Peace Commission were sent to the Bosque Redondo and talked to our leaders. Our chief spokesman, Barboncito, succeeded in convincing the Commissioners that the Navajos should be allowed to return to the lands they formerly occupied.

At a council convened on May 28, 1868, General William T. Sherman asked the Navajos to express themselves concerning the Bosque Redondo. Barboncito (pictured at left) spoke on behalf of all our people: "The bringing of us here has caused a great decrease of our numbers. Many of us have died, also a great number of our animals. Our grandfathers had no idea of living in any other country except our own and I do not think it right for us to do so . . . This ground we were brought on, it is not productive; we plant but it does not yield; all the stock we brought here have nearly all died. Because we were brought here, we have done all that we could possibly do, but found it to be labor in vain . . . There are a great many among us who were once well off, now they have nothing in their houses to sleep on except gunny sacks . . . For that reason my mouth is dry, and my head hangs in sorrow to see those around me who were at one time well off so poor now . . . It seems that whatever we do here causes death.

I hope therefore that the General will do all he can for the Indians; this hope goes in at my feet and out at my mouth . . . and I wish you to tell me when you are going to take us to our own country".

After two days of negotiations, the Commissioners and our headmen came to an agreement. The lands of the Chuska mountains were to be ours again. An agency would be established at the site of old Ft. Defiance and our herds of livestock would be replenished.

Barboncito again spoke: "That is the way I like to be and return the Commissioners my best thanks. After we get back to our country it will brighten up again and the Navajos will be as happy as the land. Black Clouds will rise and there will be plenty of rain. Corn will grow in abundance, and everything look happy".

Accordingly, on June 1, the Treaty was signed by 29 of our headmen and 10 representatives of the U. S. Government.

1

This military post, situated on the east bank of the Pecos River, lay about 165 miles southeast of Santa Fe, New Mexico. It was named in honor of General Edwin Voss Sumner, a cavalry officer who had served in the Southwest prior to the Civil War. The post's complement consisted of some 400 soldiers from Companies of the 5th U.S. Infantry and 1st. New Mexico Infantry. Post Commanders were Major Henry D. Wallen (1864),

Brigadier General Marcellus Crocker (1865); Maj. William McCleave (1865); Lt. Col. George Sykes (1866); and Maj. Charles Whiting (1867). In November 1867, supervision of the Navajos was transferred from the military to the Superintendent of Indian Affairs. Appointed as Agent was Theodore H. Dodd who soon proved to be a very capable administrator and friend of the Navajos.

A gathering of Navajo warriors. Several of them are wearing the striped blankets which were popular with Navajo weavers of that day. In his status report for 30 May 1868, Navajo Agent Theodore Dodd stated; "The Navajos are no doubt the best in the country for rapid progress in agriculture as history proves that for several centuries they have been engaged in planting and that they are far in advance of other tribes in manufacturing blankets, bridles and other articles."

Navajo dwellings were woefully inadequate at the Bosque Redondo. The people would dig round holes in the ground, as deep as possible without the earthen walls caving in. Then these holes were roofed over with branches, brush, scraps of canvas, and sometimes cow or buffalo hides. It was in damp, drafty and ill-heated "cellars" such as these that most of the Navajos (but not all) managed to survive four harsh and severe winters.

Issue of rations at Ft. Sumner. In spite of hard work and a determined effort to develop farms in the valley of the Rio Pecos, the annual crop yield was usually far below the minimum needs of the people. Cut worm, floods, hailstorms, drought, and alkaline soil all contributed to crop failures. As a result the Government was forced to issue rations to prevent widespread starvation. Between 1864 and 1868 the U. S. Government expended over 10 million dollars on supplies and food-stuffs for the 7,000 Navajos at Bosque Redondo.

A street scene in Ft. Sumner during the 1860's. The post was established in October 1862, as the headquarters for the Bosque Redondo Indian Reservation. The first Indians to arrive were some 400 Mescalero Apaches from southeastern New Mexico. Most of the adobe buildings were constructed by work forces comprised of both soldiers, Mescalero Apaches, and Navajos. By the end of 1864 the post included barracks, corrals and stables, officer's quarters, administration buildings, warehouses, hospital, sutler's store, commissary, laundry, bakery and a blacksmithy.

A group of Navajos in front of the Provost Marshal's Office. The Provost Marshal was responsible for issuing passes to Navajos who wished to travel away from the post. For the most part, however, this system was ineffectual, as many would leave without the formalities of obtaining a pass and the Army was constantly sending out patrols to bring these recalcitrant Navajos back. On February 1, 1868, it was reported that during the month of January, 250 to 300 Navajos left the post. The report continued, "the Indians are very much dissatisfied as we have had a very severe winter thus far and they are suffering very much from the want of firewood".

TREATY BETWEEN THE UNITED STATES OF AMERICA AND THE NAVAJO TRIBE OF INDIANS

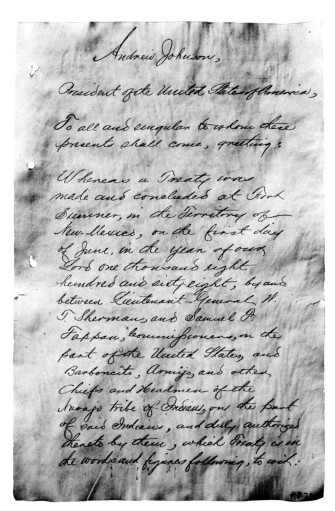

Articles of a Treaty and Agreement made and entered into at Fort Sumner, New Mexico, on the first day of June, 1868, by and between the United States, represented by its Commissioners, Lieutenant General W. T. Sherman and Colonel Samuel F. Tappan, of the one part, and the Navajo nation or tribe of Indians, represented by their Chiefs and Headmen, duly authorized and empowered to act for the whole people of said nation or tribe, (the names of said Chiefs and Headmen being hereto subscribed,) of the other part, witness:

Article I.

From this day forward all war between the parties to this agreement shall for ever cease. The government of the United States desires peace, and its honor is hereby pledged to keep it. The Indians desire peace, and they now pledge their honor to keep it.

If bad men among the whites, or among other people subject to the authority of the United States, shall commit any wrong upon the person or property of the Indians, the United States will, upon proof made to the agent and forwarded to the Commissioner of Indian Affairs at Washington city, proceed at once to cause the offender to be arrested and punished according to the laws of the United States, and also to reimburse the injured persons for the loss sustained.

If bad men among the Indians shall commit a wrong or depredation upon the person or property of any one, white, black, or Indian, subject to the authority of the United States and at peace therewith, the Navajo tribe agree that they will, on proof made to their agent, and on notice by him, deliver up the wrongdoer to the United States, to be tried and punished according to its laws; and in case they wilfully refuse so to do, the person injured shall be reimbursed for his loss from the annuities or other moneys due or to become due them under this treaty, or any others that may be made with the United States. And the President may prescribe such rules and regulations for ascertaining damages under this article as in his judgment may be proper; but no such damage shall be adjusted and paid until examined and passed upon by the Commissioner of Indian Affairs, and no one sustaining loss whilst violating, or because of his violating, the provisions of this treaty or the laws of the United States, shall be reimbursed therefor.

Article II.

The United States agrees that the following district of country, to wit: bounded on the north by the 37th degree of north latitude, south by an east and west line passing through the site of old Fort Defiance, in Canon Bonito, east by the parallel of longitude which, if prolonged south, would pass through old Fort Lyon, or the Ojo-de-oso, Bear Spring and west by a parallel of longitude 109° 30' west of Greenwich, provided it embraces the outlet of the Canon-de-Chilly, which canon is to be all included in this reservation, shall be, and the same is hereby, set apart for the use and occupation of the Navajo tribe of Indians, and for such other friendly tribes or individual Indians as from time to time they may be willing, with the consent of the United States, to admit among them; and the United States agrees that no persons except those herein so authorized to do, and except such officers, soldiers, agents, and employes of the government, or of the Indians, as may be authorized to enter upon Indian reservations in discharge of duties imposed by law, or the orders of the President, shall ever be permitted to pass over, settle upon, or reside in, the territory described in this article.

Article III.

The United States agrees to cause to be built at some point within said reservation, where timber and water may be convenient, the following buildings: a warehouse, to cost not exceeding twenty-five hundred dollars; an agency building for the residence of the agent, not to cost exceeding three thousand dollars; a carpenter shop and blacksmith shop, not to cost exceeding one thousand dollars each; and a school-house and chapel, so soon as a sufficient number of children can be induced to attend school, which shall not cost to exceed five thousand dollars.

Article IV.

The United States agrees that the agent for the

Navajos shall make his home at the agency building; that he shall reside among them and shall keep an office open at all times for the purpose of prompt and diligent inquiry into such matters of complaint by or against the Indians as may be presented for investigation, as also for the faithful discharge of other duties enjoined by law. In all cases of depredation on person or property he shall cause the evidence to be taken in writing and forwarded, together with his finding, to the Commissioner of Indian Affairs, whose decision shall be binding on the parties to this treaty.

Article V.

If any individual belonging to said tribe, or legally incorporated with it, being the head of a family, shall desire to commence farming, he shall have the privilege to select, in the presence and with the assistance of the agent then in charge, a tract of land within said reservation, not exceeding one hundred and sixty acres in extent, which tract, when so selected, certified, and recorded in the "land book" as herein described, shall cease to be held in common, but the same may be occupied and held in the exclusive possession of the person selecting it, and of his family, so long as he or they may continue to cultivate it.

Any person over eighteen years of age, not being the head of the family, may in like manner select, and cause to be certified to him or her for purposes of cultivation, a quantity of land, not exceeding eighty acres in extent, and thereupon be entitled to the exclusive possssion of the same as above directed.

For each tract of land so selected a certificate containing a description thereof, and the name of the person selecting it, with a certificate endorsed thereon that the same has been recorded, shall be delivered to the party entitled to it by the agent, after the same shall have been recorded by him in a book to be kept in his office, subject to inspection which said book shall be known as the "Navajo Land Book."

The President may at any time order a survey of the reservation, and, when so surveyed, Congress shall provide for protecting the rights of said settlers in their improvements, and may fix the character of the title held by each. The United States may pass such laws on the subject of alienation and descent of property between the Indians and their descendants as may be thought proper.

Article VI.

In order to insure the civilization of the Indians entering into this treaty, the necessity of education is admitted, especially of such of them as may be settled on said agricultural parts of this reservation, and they therefore pledge themselves to compel their children, male and female, between the ages of six and sixteen years, to attend school; and it is hereby made the duty of the agent for said Indians to see that this stipulation is strictly complied with; and the United States agrees that, for every thirty children between said ages who can be induced or compelled to attend school, a house shall be provided, and a teacher competent to teach the elementary branches of an English education shall be furnished, who will reside among said Indians, and faithfully discharge his or her duties as a teacher.

The provisions of this article to continue for not less than ten years.

Article VII

When the head of a family shall have selected lands and received his certificate as above directed, and the agent shall be satisfied that he intends in good faith to commence cultivating the soil for a living, he shall be entitled to receive seeds and agricultural implements for the first year, not exceeding in value one hundred dollars,

and for each succeeding year he shall be entitled to receive seeds and implements to the value of twenty-five dollars.

Article VIII.

In lieu of all sums of money or other annuities provided to be paid to the Indians herein named under any treaty or treaties heretofore made, the United States agrees to deliver at the agency house on the reservation herein named, on the first day of September of each year for ten years, the following articles, to wit:

Such articles of clothing, goods, or raw materials in lieu thereof, as the agent may make his estimate for, not exceeding in value five dollars per Indian—each Indian being encouraged to manufacture their own clothing, blankets, &c.; to be furnished with no article which they can manufacture themselves. And, in order that the Commissioner of Indian Affairs may be able to estimate properly for the articles herein named, it shall be the duty of the agent each year to forward to him a full and exact census of the Indians, on which the estimate from year to year can be based.

And in addition to the articles herein named, the sum of ten dollars for each person entitled to the beneficial effects of this treaty shall be annually appropriated for a period of ten years, for each person who engages in farming or mechanical pursuits, to be used by the Commissioner of Indian Affairs in the purchase of such articles as from time to time the condition and necessities of the Indians may indicate to be proper; and if within the ten years at any time it shall appear that the amount of money needed for clothing, under the article, can be appropriated to better uses for the Indians named herein, the Commissioner of Indian Affairs may change the appropriation to other purposes, but in no event shall the amount of this appropriation be withdrawn or discontinued for the period named, provided they remain at peace. And the President shall annually detail an officer of the army to be present and attest the delivery of all the goods herein named to the Indians, and he shall inspect and report on the quantity and quality of the goods and the manner of their delivery.

Article IX.

In consideration of the advantages and benefits conferred by this treaty, and the many pledges of friendship by the United States, the tribes who are parties to this agreement hereby stipulate that they will relinquish all right to occupy any territory outside their reservation, as herein defined, but retain the right to hunt on any unoccupied lands contiguous to their reservation, so long as the large game may range thereon in such numbers as to justify the chase; and they, the said Indians, further expressly agree:

1st. That they will make no opposition to the construction of railroads now being built or hereafter to be built, across the continent.

2nd. That they will not interfere with the peaceful construction of any railroad not passing over their reservation as herein defined.

3rd. That they will not attack any persons at home or travelling, nor molest or disturb any wagon trains, coaches, mules or cattle belonging to the people of the United States, or to persons friendly therewith.

4th. That they will never capture or carry off from the settlements women or children.

5th. They will never kill or scalp white men, nor attempt to do them harm.

6th. They will not in future oppose the construction of railroads, wagon roads, mail stations, or other works of utility or necessity which may be ordered or permitted by the laws of the United States; but should such roads or other works be constructed on the lands of their reservation, the government will pay the tribe whatever amount of damage may be assessed by three distinterested commissioners to be appointed by the President for that purpose, one of said commissioners to be a chief or head man of the tribe.

7th. They will make no opposition to the military posts or roads now established, or that may be established, not in violation of treaties heretofore made or hereafter to be made with any of the Indian tribes.

Article X.

No future treaty for the cession of any portion or part of the reservation herein described, which may be held in common, shall be of any validity or force against said Indians unless agreed to and executed by at least three-fourths of all the adult male Indians occupying or interested in the same; and no cession by the tribe shall be understood or construed in such manner as to deprive, without his consent, any individual member of the tribe of his rights to any tract of land selected by him as provided in article 5 of this treaty.

Article XI.

The Navajos also hereby agree that at any time after the signing of these presents they will proceed in such manner as may be required of them by the agent, or by the officer charged with their removal, to the reservation herein provided for, the United States paying for their subsistence en route, and providing a reasonable amount of transportation for the sick and feeble.

Article XII.

It is further agreed by and between the parties to this agreement that the sum of one hundred and fifty thousand dollars appropriated or to be appropriated shall be disbursed as follows, subject to any conditions provided in the law, to wit:

1st. The actual cost of the removal of the tribe from the Bosque Redondo reservation to the reservation, say fifty thousand dollars.

2nd. The purchase of fifteen thousand sheep and goats, at a cost not to exceed thirty thousand dollars.

3rd. The purchase of five hundred beef cattle and a million pounds of corn, to be collected and held at the military post nearest the reservation, subject to the orders of the agent, for the relief of the needy during the coming winter.

4th. The balance, if any, of the appropriation to be invested for the maintenance of the Indians pending their removal, in such manner as the agent who is with them may determine.

5th. The removal of this tribe to be made under the supreme control and direction of the military commander of the Territory of New Mexico, and when completed, the management of the tribe to revert to the proper agent.

Article XIII.

The tribe herein named, by their representatives, parties to this treaty, agree to make the reservation herein described their permanent home, and they will not as a tribe make any permanent settlement elsewhere, reserving the right to hunt on the lands adjoining the said reservation formerly called theirs, subject to the modifications named in this treaty and the orders of the commander of the department in which said reservation may be for the time being; and it is further agreed and understood by the parties to this treaty, that if any Navajo Indian or Indians shall leave the reservation herein described to settle elsewhere, he or they shall forfeit all the rights, privileges, and annuities conferred by the terms of this treaty; and it is further agreed by the parties to

this treaty, that they will do all they can to induce Indians now away from reservations set apart for the exclusive use and occupation of the Indians, leading a nomadic life, or engaged in war against the people of the United States, to abandon such life and settle permanently in one of the territorial reservations set apart for the exclusive use and occupation of the Indians.

In testimony of all which the said parties have hereto, on this the first day of June, eighteen hundred and sixty-eight, at Fort Sumner, in the Territory of New Mexico, set their hands and seals.

W. T. SHERMAN
Lt. Gen'l, Indian Peace Commissioner.
S. F. TAPPAN,
Indian Peace Commissioner.

BARBONCITO, Chief.	his x mark.
ARMIJO.	his x mark.
DELGADO.	
MANUELITO.	his x mark.
LARGO.	his x mark.
HERRERO.	his x mark.
CHIQUETO.	his x mark.
MUERTO DE HOMBRE.	his x mark.
HOMBRO.	his x mark.
NARBONO.	his x mark.
NARBONO SEGUNDO.	his x mark.
GANADO MUCHO.	his x mark.
Council.	
RIQUO.	his x mark.
JUAN MARTIN.	his x mark.
SERGINTO.	his x mark.
GRANDE.	his x mark.
INOETENITO	his x mark.
MUCHACHOS MUCHO.	his x mark.
CHIQUETO SEGUNDO.	his x mark.
CABELLO AMARILLO	his x mark.
FRANCISCO.	his x mark.
TORIVIO.	his x mark.
DESDENDADO.	his x mark.
JUAN.	his x mark.
GUERO.	his x mark.
GUGADORE.	his x mark.
CABASON.	his x mark.
BARBON SEGUNDO.	his x mark.
CABARES COLORADOS	his x mark.

Attest:
Geo. W. G. Getty,
Col. 37th Inf'y, Bt. Maj. Gen'l U. S. A.
B. S. Roberts,
Bt. Brg. Gen'l U. S. A., Lt. Col. 3d Cav'y.
J. Cooper Mckee,
Bt. Lt. Col. Surgeon U. S. A.
Theo. H. Dodd,
U. S. Indian Ag't for Navajos.
Chas. McClure,
Bt. Maj. and C. S. U. S. A.
James F. Weeds,
Bt. Maj. and Asst. Surg. U. S. A.
J. C. Sutherland,
Interpreter
William Vaux,
Chaplain U. S. A.

And whereas, the said treaty having been submitted to the Senate of the United States for its constitutional action thereon, the Senate did, on the twenty-fifth day of July, one thousand eight hundred and sixty-eight, advise and consent to the ratification of the same, by a resolution in the words and figures following, to wit:

Read 29, July, Mr Jefferson

In Executive Session,
Senate of the United States
July 25, 1868.

Resolved, (two thirds of the Senators present concurring,) that the Senate advise and consent to the ratification of the Treaty between the United States and the Navajo Indians, concluded at Fort Sumner, New Mexico, on the first day of June, 1868.

Attest:

Geo C. Gorham
Secretary.

by C.W.F. McDonald
Chief Clerk

Now, therefore, be it known that I, Andrew Johnson, President of the United States of America, do, in pursuance of the advice and consent of the Senate, as expressed in its resolution of the twenty-fifth of July, one thousand eight hundred and sixty-eight, accept, ratify, and confirm the said Treaty.

In testimony whereof I have hereto signed my name, and caused the seal of the United States to be affixed.

Done at the City of Washington this twelfth day of August, in the year of our Lord one thousand eight hundred and sixty-eight, and of the Independence of the United States of America the ninety-third.

Andrew Johnson

By the President:
W. Hunter,
Acting Secretary of State.

EXODUS

Farther on, he arrives with me;
From there to where my hogan first comes in sight,
Hashje-Altye arrives with me,
Whirling his dark staff about himself for protection;
Blue, small birds sing before me,
Cornbeetle sings behind me,
As Hashje-Altye arrives with me;
As the rainbow arrives at that place with me,
And the talking KEHTAHN teaches me,
Hashje-Altye arrives with me.

Homeward bound at last! After the signing of the Treaty with the representatives of the United States, our people packed their meager belongings in the available Army wagons; loaded provisions on the few mules and horses left, and carried other bundles on their backs. What excitement and expectations must have risen in the hearts of the Navajos as, on the morning of June 15, 1868, our Exodus began back to that happy land that Barboncito spoke of; back to that land between the four sacred mountains.

At Shashbito, where the Army had built Ft. Lyon, and then renamed it Wingate, we camped for the rest of the summer. During this time, surveyors marked off our reservation and the old buildings at Ft. Defiance (Canby) were refurbished and established as the new Navajo Agency (Drawing at left shows Ft. Defiance as it was before the exile to Bosque Redondo).

Theodore Dodd, who had been the Navajo agent at Ft. Sumner, took up residence at Ft. Defiance in November, 1868, and soon families were spreading out over the country side, eager to find their old homes and resettle before the heavy snows set in. When our people returned, they brought back with them only 1,500 horses and mules and 2,000 sheep and goats. The government, by terms of the Treaty, promised to issue us 15,000 sheep and goats so that we could rebuild our herds. This was accomplished during the next two years and it was good to see some of the families begin to prosper. But there was still much to be done. Long-neglected fields had to be cultivated again. Homes and corrals had to be rebuilt. Springs and water holes needed to be cleaned out. And above all, prayer-songs to the Holy Ones must once again be performed.

The years that followed were hard years, but this time our labor was not in vain. Soon, however our needs were greater than the land could support and in 1878 an executive order restored to us the western region of the Chinle valley. By January 1880, a strip 15 miles wide running north to south along the eastern boundary of the reservation was given back to us. In 1882, a large section of land, to the west, was set aside for both the Hopi and the Navajo, and in 1884 all the land in southern Utah, below the San Juan river was restored to our people.

By 1883 our numbers had risen to 19,000. We owned 35,000 horses, 200,000 goats, and more than 1,000,000 sheep. For the first time, raw wool was exported to eastern markets and over 1,000,000 pounds of it was sold at 7c to 10c per pound.

During the 1880's, four of our headmen rose in prominence and became very influential, both in Tribal affairs and in our relationships with the American government. These highly-respected Nataani were Francisco Capitan, from the San Juan area; Manuelito, who lived east of Ft. Defiance; Mariano, who resided near Ft. Wingate; and Ganado Mucho, whose home was in the Chinle Valley. But soon other names would be talked about, — names like Henry Chee Dodge, Charlie Mitchell, and Dugal Chee Bekiss.

And then the railroad came. We had promised in the Treaty not to molest the building of the railroad, but this was a very hard promise to keep. As the tracks progressed beyond Ft. Wingate into the Valley of the Rio Puerco many of our watering places and good pasture lands were taken from us. But the railroad brought us jobs, and soon too, our sheep were being sent to eastern markets. Trading centers materialized along the road and it wasn't long before bolts of cloth, tools, farm implements and even canned food found their way into every Navajo hogan.

A group of Navajo men at Ft. Defiance with William F. M. Arny. During the 1860's Arny served as acting Governor of New Mexico and in 1867 was appointed agent to the Ute and Pueblo Indians. After the murder of Navajo Agent James Miller in 1872, Thomas Keam acted as Special Agent until September 1, 1873, when Arny officially assumed charge of the Agency. The following year, Arny contrived to exchange lands along the San Juan River for less equitable lands to the east. This scheme was thwarted, and Arny was forced to resign in August, 1875.

This 1879 photo by John Hillers shows some of the earliest buildings, made of adobe and rough-cut lumber, at Ft. Defiance. When it was reoccupied upon the return from Ft. Sumner many of the original buildings were repaired and remodeled to fit the new Agency. What was once a parade ground for troops of dragoons and infantry, became an assembly area and meeting place for the Navajos visiting the Post and sutler's store.

Ganado Mucho, or Much Cattle, was recognized as head of the western bands living in the Kinlichee - Chinle Valley region. He was born sometime around 1809, although the year is not certain. His family was among the first to go to Ft. Sumner, where one of his sons was killed during a Commanche raid. He was considered a Peace Chief and sought constantly to bring about better relationships and a reconciliation betweeen his people and the Anglo-American. He died during the winter of 1893-94.

The years following the return from Bosque Redondo were hard years, especially the winters. Orchards and cornfields, left abandoned, had deteriorated into empty sand dunes. According to the Treaty the Government was to furnish the head of each family with $100.00 worth of seed and farm implements with which to rebuild their farmlands. To some extent, seeds were distributed during the spring of 1869, but it was several years before farm tools, hoes, and wagons were made available to the Navajo. Agent Theodore Dodd was only the first of a succession of agents who found that the procurement of necessary supplies and rations to be one of their biggest, but not insurmountable problems.

For ten years after the Treaty, the Government was under obligation to provide the basic necessities of life to the Navajo people. Sustenance, in the form of beef, flour, coffee and salt were hauled in from Albuquerque, and distributed on Saturdays from the warehouses at Ft. Defiance. On special occasions the people received tobacco and sugar. The Navajo picked up food habits in those ration days which, in some areas, have persisted to the present. Clothing, too, was greatly influenced during this period when each person received an annual allotment of $5.00 worth of materials. Ready-made clothing was also available, when in 1870, the Government issued $40,000 worth of shirts, trousers, coats, and women's garments. A few years later blankets manufactured in Pendleton, Oregon, began to replace the handwoven Navajo blanket and buckskin soon gave way to flour sack material, unbleached muslin, blue and white striped denim and figured calico.

Ft. Defiance in the 1880's. Constantly changing, the Post by now had taken on a new appearance with the construction of the three-storey school building on the left. The fort was the first American military post in Arizona, being established on September 18, 1851, by Colonel Edwin V. Sum-

ner, commander of the Ninth Military Department. The site, called by the Navajos TSE HOOT-SOI (Meadow between the rocks), and by the early Spaniards, Canyon Bonito, was selected because of its plentiful supply of forage and water. During the 1850's several campaigns against the

Navajos were conducted from this Post; most were failures, some resulted in ineffectual and unkept treaties. An unforgettable experience for the Navajos occurred in August, 1857, when Lt. Edward F. Beale arrived at the Post with a caravan of camels and Arabian camel-drivers, while on his trail-blazing expedition from San Antonio, Texas to California. On April 30, 1860, over 1000 Navajos attacked the Post and were driven off only after a bloody two-hour engagement. On April 28, 1861, Ft. Defiance was abandoned but reoccupied by Carson's troops in July, 1863.

Fort Wingate in 1893. Originally established as Ft. Fauntleroy in August, 1860, it served as Infantry support to Ft. Defiance. When its namesake, Colonel Thomas Fauntleroy, resigned his commission in 1861, to join the Confederacy, the post was renamed Ft. Lyon. Later that year, the garrison was withdrawn to the Rio Grande to bolster troops confronting the invading Confederate forces from Texas. In 1868, upon the return of the Navajos from Ft. Sumner, the miliary post at San Rafael, named Ft. Wingate was abandoned and the garrison moved west to reoccupy Ft. Lyon, which in turn was renamed Ft. Wingate. The post was evacuated in 1912, but then reoccupied by the Ordnance Department in 1918.

Looking south across Fort Defiance sometime in the 1890's. By this time the Post had developed into a substantial community and buildings of a permanent nature had been constructed. Ever since its establishment as the Agency in November, 1868, the Post was the center of all Navajo activity. The civilian agents in charge found their job to be anything but dull and several times troops had to be called from Ft. Wingate to quell minor disturbances. However, by diligent work and a conscientious effort by both sides, achievements were made and soon Ft. Defiance became known as the Cradle of Navajo Progress. It was here that rations, annuities, sheep and goats were issued to the people to help rebuild their economy. It was Ft. Defiance that became the site of the first day school (1869), the first mission(1871), the first boarding school (1883), first hospital (1897), and first public school for the Navajos (1954).

At left, a studio portrait of Manuelito Segundo, the son of Chief Manuelito and his wife Juanita. The photo was taken in Washinton, D.C. in 1874, while he was member of the delegation brought to that city by Agent W. F. Arny. Early in 1874 several Navajos were killed in southern Utah and the blame placed on local Mormons. Arny used this episode to convince the Commissioner of Indian Affairs that open warfare was eminent on the northern boundary of the reservation. In August, 1874, the Commissioners finally agreed to authorize Arny to accompany a delegation of Navajo headmen to Washington. Arny's real motive, however, was to effect a land exchange by ceding the northern portion of the reservation bordering the San Juan River, where gold seekers

were beginning to stake claims, for parcels of arid lands to the east and west. President Grant met with the delegation on December 10, but the land exchange fell through, due mainly to the efforts of Thomas Keam who had travelled to Washington at his own expense and shared the Navajos' desire to hold onto their lands. The delegation consisted of (left to right, front row) Carnero Mucho, Mariano, Juanita (Manuelito's wife), Manuelito, Manuelito Segundo, and Tiene-su-se. Standing are "Wild" Hank Sharp (Anglo), Ganado Mucho, Barbas Hueros, Agent William Arny, Kentucky Mountain Bill (Anglo), Cabra Negra, Cayatanita, Narbona Primero, and Jesus Arviso, interpreter.

Carnero Mucho (above), a Navajo captain and member of the delegation to Washington in 1874, along with Mariano (below). Manuelito (right), most noted of all the Navajo headmen, was born around 1819 and died of pneumonia in February, 1894. In his later years he worked hard to further the cause of the Navajo and his position as head NAAT'AANI was recognized by both the Navajo and Anglo alike.

A group studio portrait of three Navajo headmen. Tiene-su-se (left) was third war chief at the time. Ganado Mucho (his Navajo name was Tot'-sonii Hastiin) stands in the center and on the right, Mariano, second war chief. Mariano lived north and east of Ft. Wingate and helped the survey party lay out the original reservation boundary. In 1886, along with Manuelito, he recruited Navajo scouts for service in the Apache campaign. In the photo, note the deerskin trousers of Gando Mucho and the buckskin leggings with silver buttons.

23

A NEW BEGINNING

"This is your home, my Grandchild!"
He says to me as he sits down beside me;
my grandchild!"
"I have returned with you to your home,
He says to me as he sits down beside me;
"Upon the pollen figure I have returned
to sit with you, my grandchild!"
He says to me as he sits down beside me;
"Your home is yours again —"
"Your fire is yours again —"
"Your food is yours again —"
"Your mountain ranges are yours again,
my grandchild,"
He says to me as he sits down beside me.

It was our herds of sheep that had become the backbone of our livelihood. The welfare and maintenance of our flocks became our chief occupation, and it wasn't many years after the return from Ft. Sumner that thousands of sheep, goats, and horses were grazing from the San Juan to the Little Colorado; from the Valley of the Rio Chaco to the Grand Canyon. Many families ranged outside the confining boundaries of the reservation but on lands historically belonging to the Navajo — those lands between the Four Sacred Mountains. Theirs was a hard lot and their freedom, their will to survive, was constantly being challenged.

One deplorable episode occured in Coconino county in early 1897 and was reported by W. A. Jones, Commissioner of Indian Affairs: "In January there were 16 Navajo families tending their flocks in a grazing district bounded on the west by the Colorado river . . . a tract of country which they had thus occupied for generations and which has never been surveyed . . . On January 19, the sheriff with an armed posse visited each of these 16 families and demanded that $5.00 for every 100 sheep owned by them be paid to him at once; failing to do so they were to move out immediately. The Navajo had no money; their prayer for time in which to procure money or to ascertain their rights was denied, and in default of the payment of the arbitrary and unlawful sum fixed by the sheriff, the Indians were forced to gather up their belongings and move.

"Snow was falling, the weather was bitter cold, and the ewes were lambing. The Indians pleaded for a reasonable time within which to remove, but were denied. Their houses and corrals were burned and they and their flocks were rounded up and pushed north toward the Little Colorado River with relentless haste, the posse keeping women, children, and animals in a fright by an intermittent fire from rifles and revolvers. When the river was reached it was found to be so deep as to require the sheep to swim. The posse surrounded the flocks and pushed them into the water, and nearly all the lambs, with many grown sheep, went down the stream or froze to death after crossing, and many died afterward from the effects of exposure".

In spite of adversities such as this, most families prospered and continued to increase their herds. In 1915, a census was taken of the Ft. Defiance Agency (by this time additional agencies had been established for the San Juan, Pueblo Bonito, Western area, and at Leupp), an area of 3,000,000 acres and occupied by 11,915 persons. The report showed 406,316 sheep, 116,202 goats, 26,255 horses, and 14,406 cattle. Three billion feet of merchantable timber were valued at $7,500,000.00 and known coal deposits had an estimated value of several million more dollars. By this time, schools were operating at Ft. Defiance (430 students), Chinle (200 students), St. Michaels (160), Tohatchi (150), Lukachukai (60), Rehoboth (60), Ganado Mission (40), and Cornfields (30 day students).

The census also listed the Navajos who were proud owners of that new invention — the automobile. Chee Dodge owned a Dodge, and Tom Damon, Willie Damon, Hosteen Yazza, and Clitsoi Dedman all possessed Fords.

We were growing in numbers, growing in wealth, and growing 'in land — in 1886, 40,000 acres south of the San Juan was restored, and in 1900, 1,517,785 acres west of the 1882 extension were also given back to us. The following year an Executive Order added the 419,622 acre Leupp sector to the Navajo Reservation.

But over this land Black Clouds were forming, and officials from Washington were using new and ominous words, like land depletion, erosion, and — stock reduction.

James Mooney took this photo of the three children of Pesh-lakai-ilhini during his trip to the Navajo Reservation in the winter of 1892-93. Children, for the most part wore the same styles of clothing as did their parents, being commonly manufactured from the calico and muslin which was first issued as annuities and then later available at the trading posts.

Pedro and Anrelina, two Navajos photographed by Ben Wittick, probably in the 1880's. Dressed in their finest, they depict the Navajo mode of dress in the 19th Century. Pedro wears the typical V-necked shirt, without collar, made of printed calico. The white muslin trousers are loose fitting and split up the sides — reminiscent of the type worn by early Spanish caballeros. The moccasins and leggings are fashioned from buckskin and dyed red. When worn, the leggings, as well as the blue knit stockings underneath, are held in place just below the knee by a brightly colored woven garter. Pedro wears a revolver and holds a double-barrel percussion shotgun. Anrelina wears the traditional biil or woven woolen dress. The style was copied from the Pueblo dress which was being worn when the Spaniards entered the Southwest. The Pueblo dress, however, was of native cotton and woven as one piece. The Navajo woman wove hers in two separate pieces and then fastened them together, leaving spaces at the top and sides as openings for the head and arms. With this dress the women wore leggings of tanned buckskin, the skin being attached to the moccasin and then wrapped around the leg from ankle to knee.

A group of Navajos who had served as scouts with the Army during the Geronimo Campaign, 1872-1886. The photo was taken some years later, probably at the time they each received the Indian Campaign medal. This medal, authorized by Congress in 1876, consisted of a bronze medal-lion on a red and black ribbon and was awarded to those who served with valor and courage. This ribbon can be seen on the left chest of the men in the picture. Their names are, (1) Calavasa, (2) George, (3) Chatsosee, (4) Nastagi, (5) Naschi, (6) Frank Taylor, (7) Casa Miri, (8) Slim Jim,

Chich-is-nez, sub-chief of Navajo scouts serving with the U.S. Army during the Apache campaigns. At the outbreak of hostilities with the various Apache groups to the south, the Commanding Officer of Ft. Wingate was directed to recruit Navajos to serve as scouts and interpreters. Chiefs Manuelito, Barbon Cito, and Mariano travelled throughout the Navajo country and, with the promise of additional grants of land, induced nearly 200 Navajos to serve with the Cavalry.

A total of four platoons, with Anglo officers and non-coms were organized and mustered into service at Ft. Wingate.

(9) Navaho Tom, (10) Hosteen Nez, (11) Mosto, (12) As Keen Nez - zy, (13) Sombrero Ancho, (14) Atcitty Spahe, (15) Guerito, (16) Charley No. 1, (17) Palo Cosa, (18) Quintana, (19) Canuco Pinto, (20) Don Juan, (31) Wooly Willie, (22) Mike, (23) Navaho John, (24) Apachito, (25) Sam Nelson, (26) Dine Chili, (27) Woolto, (28) Jack, (29) Francisco, (30) Marianito, (31) Choiska, (32) Maya, (33) Moqui, (34) Biga, (35) Pinto, (36) Charley Chiquito, (37) Bicente.

This studio portrait shows three of the Navajo scouts who served in southern Arizona and New Mexico during the Apache campaigns from 1872-1886. From left to right, Pedro, Gayetenito, and Cis Biziz.

30

Black Horse and Taiyoni. Black Horse was a leader of a band of very traditionally-minded Navajos in the Round Rock area and for years he vigorously opposed the policy of sending Navajo children off to the boarding school at Ft. Defiance. Matters came to a head in late October, 1892, when Agent Dana Shipley and an escort of Navajo police arrived at Round Rock for the express purpose of compelling the children to accompany them back to Ft. Defiance. A fist fight developed and Shipley was forced to take refuge in the trading post. Two days later a cavalry escort came to their rescue.

The photo at left, of Hashke Yazhe, portrays the age-old dignity of the Navajo horseman. Nomadic since earliest times, the Navajo and their linguistic cousins, the Apaches, readily adapted the horse into their culture soon after it was introduced into the Southwest by the Spaniards. These Athabaskans had long roamed throughout the Southwest and were probably the "Querechos" referred to by Coronado in 1541. Later Spanish expeditions recognized the similarity of dialect among these roving groups and classified them all as "Apaches" (derived from the Zuni word "Apachu", meaning stranger or enemy). The horse soon became a valuable asset to the nomadic and warlike tendencies of these Apache groups, enabling them to move swifter, farther, and easier than they could ever do on foot. Navajo ponies were usually small, fleet, sure-footed, and enduring. Like the sheep, they are no beauties, but natural selection has developed a strain with the ability to survive in this arid land. There is probably not another tribe in the Southwest which even today uses horses more than the Navajo.

Navajo silversmith near Tohatchi working at his anvil. Behind him is the charcoal hearth and bellows used for melting either raw silver or coins into workable disks or bands. An array of handmade stamps and dies lie in the foreground. Silver smithing is a relatively recent craft among the Navajos and did not become widely known until after the return from Ft. Sumner. One of the first smiths, Atsidi Sani, had learned the craft from some itinerent Mexicans but worked mainly with iron and copper. During the 1870's he and his sons began to manufacture simple bracelets, tobacco flasks, small bells, and bridle ornaments from silver. Atsidi Chon is credited with being the first silversmith, in 1880, to set turquoise in silver. The commercialization of the craft began in 1899, when the Fred Harvey Company started to order silver articles made up expressly for Anglo consumption. Today, Navajo silverwork is manufactured mainly by casting, hammering, or overlay and is characterized by simplicity in design and a conservative use of turquoise.

Weaving has always been, and, to some extent, still is an important function of the family. Reports on the superior quality of Navajo blankets can be found in early Spanish chronicles, and with the exception of the period of the "pound rug" at the beginning of the present century, this Navajo craft has remained unexcelled to this day. The basic techniques used are quite similar to those of the Pueblo Indians and it is assumed that the early Navajo adopted the principles of weaving from them. With the advent of Spanish sheep, wool rapidly replaced native cotton as material for both warp and weft. The top picture, taken near Keams Canyon by James Mooney in early 1893 shows members of a family performing the various stages of manufacturing a rug. The small girl in the foreground is carding wool which is then spun, by use of a hand-rotated spindle, by the woman at left. The woman at right sits beside a belt loom. The lower picture shows a Navajo family in front of a large loom.

The Treaty of 1868 stipulated that the Navajos would compel all their children, between six and sixteen years of age, to attend school; and that the Government would furnish both a classroom and a competent teacher for every thirty students. In 1869, Miss Charity Gaston was hired as teacher at Ft. Defiance but the attempt to recruit students was unsuccessful. The following year the Board of Indian Commissioners prefered the educational program for the Navajo Tribe to the Presbyterian Board of Missions, and the offer was accepted. The first teacher under this new arrangement was Mrs. Charity Menaul, wife of Dr. J. Menaul, who served as both physician and minister to the Agency. In 1880, the construction of a boarding school was commenced by the Bureau of Indian Affairs. On October 14, Agent F. T. Bennett reported that a sawmill was in operation and stone was being quarried for construction purposes, however, since only $875 was appropriated for the project, it took over two years to complete. The photo above was taken in front of the boarding school by Cosmos Mindeleff in 1893. The bearded man on the right is Agent Dana Shipley.

The above photo was taken around the turn of the century and gives a good idea of the type of disciplined life the Navajo student led. Dressed in uniforms and marched to and from classes, it was a far-different life from one of sheep tending, and, needless to say, truancy was high. As the years went by, school life improved and became more and more accepted by the Navajo. Facilities improved too; by the 1920's the Ft. Defiance school boasted of both indoor plumbing and electricity. The photo at left shows a classroom of that period. The teacher is Miss Sadie Evans.

"Return of the Bear Hunters" is the title given to this picture by Ben Wittick of a group of Navajos in front of the Thunderbird Trading Post in Chinle. Since the bear is highly regarded in Navajo religion, it is only on rare occasions that one is killed. The photo affords a good view of war equipment used by the Navajos. The man on the left is wearing a war cap, or helmet, made of the skin from the head of a mountain lion. These caps were both symbolic and protective and could be made from the skins of badgers or wildcats as well. Usually, the cap was fitted with a chin strap and decorated with eagle feathers, projectile points and bits of abalone. The same man holds a spear which is probably an adaptation of an early Spanish lance. In evidence, too, are the sinew-backed bows, a popular Navajo weapon for centuries. The arrows were made of willow and tipped with a metal point. In some instances a poison, made of rattlesnake venom and blood mixed with yucca juice, was applied to the point. Both the bow and the arrows were carried in a quiver made of a skin of a mountain lion.

The Lynch Brothers Trading Post and post office, located west of Gallup as it appeared in 1894. The early trading post played an important and significant role in the development of the Reservation during the latter part of the 19th Century. In 1868, two traders were licensed to operate stores in Ft. Defiance but by the turn of the century almost a hundred were in business through-out the region. The early traders were a mixed lot —some, second generation Santa Fe or Taos traders, a few were Mormons, driven westward by religious persecution, others like Anson Damon and Sam Day were Civil War veterans, and a rare few, like old Dan DuBois were survivors of the old mountain trade.

This interior photo of the old Lorenzo Hubbell trading post presents a graphic description of the wide variety of merchandise handled by the trader. Early posts carried just a few staples — flour, coffee, sugar, tobacco and several bolts of cloth. Later, posts expanded into all sorts of groceries, dry goods, luxuries, tools, farm implements and kitchen utensils. The store was the hub of social life and besides his regular duties of buying and selling, the trader had to be ever ready to serve as doctor, undertaker, banker, advisor, and even peacemaker in family or clan disputes. One such trader was Don Lorenzo Hubbell, who, in 1876 established his first store at Ganado, Arizona (now a National Historic Site).

The mail must go through! This early model T Ford, with only one headlight, made the mail run from Gallup, New Mexico, to the Agency at Ft. Defiance, then on to Ganado, and, weather permitting, Chinle. Post Offices were deemed important in developing the Navajo country and they were established in many isolated localities, sometimes at considerable expense. The earliest post office, not only for the Navajo reservation, but for the entire state of Arizona was established at Ft. Defiance, having opened for business on April 9, 1856. It was abandoned when the fort was abandoned in 1861 but re-established in 1868. With the coming of the railroad post offices were established at Ft. Wingate (1874), Flagstaff (1881), Gallup (1882), Holbrook (1882), and Winslow (1882). A post office was created at the Hubbell Trading Post in Ganado in 1883. Subsequent post offices were established at Keams Canyon (1883), Navajo Springs (1883), Houck (1884), Tuba City (1884), Tohatchi (1898), St. Michaels (1902), Chinle (1903), Crystal (1903), Shiprock (1904), Leupp (1905), Chambers (1907), and Kayenta (1911).

40

To keep the various trading posts supplied was not always an easy matter. Even after the railroad extended its lines along the southern boundaries of Navajoland in the 1880's, provisions, tools, and supplies had to be hauled many miles by cumbersome freight wagons. In the years immediately following the return from Ft. Sumner, the Agency and a few scattered trading posts had to rely entirely on oft-times undependable wagon caravans coming from Santa Fe or Albuquerque. With the coming of the railroad, merchantile depots were established at Gallup, Defiance Station (Manuelito), Winslow, and Flagstaff.

The Navajos' keen desire to prove his manliness and courage, once put to the test on the battlefield, was now being satisfied on the sports field. As more boarding schools were established throughout the Reservation, an inter-school sports program was developed. It soon became a most popular facet of the over-all educational program and played an exciting role in community activities. The photo above was taken of a football game in the 1920's, being played on the field adjacent to the St. Michaels Mission School. Below, on the dusty field just north of the boarding school, the home team from Ft. Defiance beat the visiting team from San Juan 19-5. The game was played in October, 1913.

The more traditional games, too, remained popular and to some extent, are still played today. In August, 1908, a large crowd watches a chicken pull at Ft. Defiance. Here Navajo horsemen pit their riding skill and agility against one another by attempting to pull a chicken from the ground while riding at a full gallup.

A gathering of Navajo families. The conical shaped forked-pole hogan becomes the focus of social activity as clan members of the family arrive for an impending ceremony. The Navajo have always been basically camp dwellers, rather than true nomads, and normally lead a life of semi-isolation, spending much of their time with their herds of sheep and goats. At the slightest provocation, however, families will get together, sometimes travelling for many miles by horseback, wagon, or pick-up.

Navajo family life has always been close knit, with everyone participating in all the household chores. The very old and the very young are

usually entrusted with the care of the flocks, tending them by day and bringing them back to the safety of the corral in the evening. Planting and cultivating are usually handled by the men and boys while cooking and other household chores fall to the women and girls. Ownership and property rights are carefully defined within a Navajo family. While the husband may own the horses and cattle, the sheep are generally the property of the wife. Weapons, saddles, and tools traditionally belong to the males and all household items and utensils, including the rugs they make, belong to the wife and daughters. Navajo families are both matrilocal and matrilineal.

Navajo religion is a combination of moral philosophy and preventive medicine. The teachings and beliefs are set forth in a myriad of legends and corresponding ceremonies. Throughout all these legends, Man is the central theme and is paramount in the Navajo world, with the sun, moon, stars, animals, plants, ceremonial knowledge, and all the rest of nature created for his use and benefit. To the Navajo, the constant purpose of life is to control his environment. He can best do this by observing various taboos and by avoiding or overcoming disease, misfortune, or evil through the proper exercise of a prescribed ceremony. At all times he must maintain, or re-establish his balance and harmony with nature. The ceremonies and rituals of Navajo religion are aimed at fulfilling the requirements of life and living; they are not concerned with preparation for death and afterlife. After death man loses his identity and merely becomes one with the universe, and is neither punished nor rewarded.

One of the major ceremonies of the Navajo is the nine-day Night Chant. It is during this ceremony that boys and girls receive their initiation into the rituals of Navajo religion. The boys are stripped to a loincloth, and with heads bowed, are approached by the masked Yeibichai who sprinkles pollen over various parts of the boy's body and then "whips" him with yucca leaves.

The Night Chant, or Yeibichai dance, is only held during the winter months and is usually attended by everyone from miles around. The top picture was taken in 1905 of just such a gathering. Notice the "Haystacks" in the background. Below it, the personator of DSAHADOLDZA, the Fringe Mouth, replete with fox skin collar, silver jewelry, kilt and leather pouch blesses the patient.

47

The begging gods, or food solicitors are first sent out on the sixth day of the ceremony. The personators dispatched are usually HASTSEYALTI, or Talking God (left), HASTESELPAHI, the Grey God (center), and HASTSEBAAD, The Female God (right). They are dressed and adorned in the ceremonial lodge, early in the morning. As soon as they are made ready, they go forth on their errands but must return by night-fall. The personators never ride horseback while in costume, only walk. When they enter a camp they speak to no one, but dance around, uttering their distinctive cries, while one of them holds out the fawn-skin bag to receive donations. When an article is offered, the solicitor does not always accept it at once, but advances and retreats four times. On the fourth advance, he opens the bag and allows the donor to put the offering into it. The gifts are usually food and tobacco for use in the lodge.

The second day of the Night Chant is a busy one. In the morning sacrificial kethawns and ceremonial cigarettes are prepared, and the patient is administered his first sweat bath. In the afternoon a small dry-painting is made and appropriate chants are sung. The dry-painting is about a yard in diameter. At the outer edge, in the four cardinal points, are four mounds of colored sand representing the four sacred mountains. The four single colored lines leading from the mountains toward the central figure indicate the trails of various gods. The figure in the center is that of THADITIN ASIKE, or Pollen Boy. Leading to the center of the painting is a line of white corn meal and in its course are figures of four foot prints. The patient is then brought in and made to exactly follow these foot steps and then sit in the center of the painting. Hastseyalti arrives and takes his place to the north of the patient and the singing and chanting commences.

A very fundamental ritual of Navajo religion is the creation and use of pictorial altars during specific ceremonies. These are often referred to as "sand paintings", but the term is misleading, since many other ingredients, besides sand, are used. The Chanter and his assistants use a variety of crushed rock, charcoal, corn meal, pollen, pulverized blossoms, and colored ochres to create the picture, usually on a base of fine sand. These holy and symbolic pictures are not spontaneous and creative expressions of the Medicine Man, but must repeat, without alteration, the traditional designs as handed down through the generations. Color is used to indicate the direc-

tions, to represent the natural or characteristic appearance of objects depicted, to suggest qualities and power, and to identify the sex of the figure shown. The cardinal directions are generally represented by white for east, blue for south, yellow for west, and black for north. Figures are usually composed of simple geometric shapes such as squares, rectangles, circles and triangles. All human and animal figures wear masks, with the circular ones indicating the male gods and the rectangular masks denoting the female gods. In most paintings, all but the eastern portion is protected by the encircling blue and red band of the Rainbow Girl.

When the drypainting is completed, the patient is brought in and seated upon it. The painting is blessed with the pollen and cornmeal offerings and therefore becomes a "holy place". The patient becomes ritually identified with the deities depicted in the painting and absorbs from the holy symbols the necessary power and strength to ward off the evil that is inflicting him. With his disease cured, he can once again live in harmony with his environment. At the conclusion of the ceremony, the drypainting is obliterated and the sand removed from the hogan.

In all Navajo ceremonies, much of the ritual, chanting, dry-painting, making of prayer sticks, and general conduct of the rite, is under the direct supervision and direction of the Medicine Man. He is a man of unusual talents and prodigious memory. His revered position as HATAATLI comes only after years of arduous study and apprenticeship, by which time he will know one of the great ceremonies perfectly, and some of the minor ones as well. The intricacies of a nine-day "Way" range from the creation of several dry-paintings to the purification rites (shown above) and the supervision of the dancers (next page). The Medicine Man shown here is the late Tonnie Zonnie Yazzie, of Naschiti.

A TIME FOR LIVING

*"From the Dark Thunder Hogan,
    kind feelings will come to you as you go
    about in life,"*
He says to me as he sits down beside me;
    "Guided by these things, you shall live on,
respected everywhere, my grandchild,"
    he says to me as he sits down beside me;
"Guided by these things, you shall find protection
    in all places as you live on, my grandchild,"
he says to me as he sits down beside me;
    "Guided by these things, people everywhere
will refuse to part with you, my grandchild,"
    he says to me as he sits down beside me.

In the shadowy realm of long ago, this land that was to be ours was plagued by all sorts of strange monsters and evil beings. They ravaged the land and would have made it impossible for the Earth People to survive here were it not for the efforts of one of the Hero Twins, Nayenezghani, or Monster Slayer, who obtained powerful weapons from his father, the Sun. With these, he was able to overcome many of the evil beings and made this land habitable for the Earth People.

However, lest we get soft and forgetful of the gods, and what they have done for us, Nayenezghani spared four of the evils which he encountered, and these are with us yet today — Old Age, Sickness, Poverty, and Death.

And so it shall be; our legacy from the past is a challenge to the present and the future. Squarely, and with determination we must answer the questions which are now on everybody's lips — How are The People to make a living? How are we to live with white Americans? What alien ways must we learn if we are to survive? How much of the old pattern of life can we safely, or even profitably preserve? These problems, basically, are not new; they were faced by our ancestors when they came into contact with the Puebloans and then the Spaniards. But the solutions must be ours alone. As our forefathers before us, we must adapt and assimilate into our culture that what we find good and useful and discard what is deemed not important or helpful.

The problems faced in the first half of this century — stock reduction, land depletion, tuberculosis, chronic unemployment, lack of roads and utilities, and many others have generally been resolved, or are being acted upon. Manuelito proposed a solution to many of our problems when he told Chee Dodge: "My grandchild, the whites have many things which we Navajos need. But we cannot get them. It is as though the whites were in a grassy canyon and there they have wagons, plows, and plenty of food. We Navajos are up on the dry mesa. We can hear them talking but we cannot get to them. My grandchild, education is the ladder. Tell our people to take it".

Chee Dodge did tell us about education, and we listened. During the administration of Sam Ahkeah, a Scholarship Fund was established to provide financial assistance to Navajos seeking a college education. A school construction program was initiated under the Paul Jones administration and accelerated during the Raymond Nakai administration. In his inaugural speech in April, 1955, Jones reiterated Manuelito when he said: "It has been stated on the Council floor that the reason for which relocation is not successful as it might be is because of the lack of education. That should inspire us to go forward. Those of you who have been educated must tell your people the benefits of education. It is the greatest hope that we have for our Navajo people".

With education has come self-government, a development which we can truly be proud of. From the local chapter meeting (pictured at left) to the chambers of the Tribal Council we have a voice in our affairs. With assistance from various Federal, State, and private agencies, we have created imaginative and far-reaching programs to combat those ancient evils of Poverty and Sickness. Many of these programs are channeled through the Office of Navajo Economic Opportunity and are being accomplished by determination and hard work — not by resorting to riots, sit-ins, and flower waving!

As we look forward to the next hundred years our goal is to build a better world; the one where every Navajo shall stand erect beside his fellow Americans as an equal among equals.

The ballot box has always been the bulwark of American democracy. The right to vote and thereby having a voice in the affairs of government is generally thought of as dating back to the very founding of our Republic. This, however, has not been so. Negroes were given the right to vote in 1868, Puerto Ricans in 1917, and women in 1920. But the First Americans were not granted this right until 1924. The photo above was taken at St. Michaels Mission in 1903, one of the first precincts in Apache County, in the Territory of Arizona. Casting his vote in the territorial election is Father Anslem Weber, who was to become renown for his strong support and backing of Navajo land claims. Guarding the ballot box is Sam E. Day, who served as election clerk. Sitting in the background wearing the hat is Frank Walker, while Dan Mitchell stands on the right.

Since 1924, Navajos have been able to vote in county, state and federal elections as well as selecting their delegates to the Tribal Council. In the 1930's only a handful of Navajos were registered and eligible to vote in non-tribal elections. Today more than 30,000 are registered voters.

Ganado Mission, some 30 miles west of Ft. Defiance is a fine example of a Christian Church's endeavor to aid and assist the Navajo. Established in 1901 by the Presbyterian Church the mission soon developed a three-fold program—evangelism, education, and medical service. The first missionary was Mr. Charles Bierkemper who built the first church while his wife taught school in one of the rooms of the Hubbell Trading Post. The first hospital was completed in 1911 under the direction of Dr. James Kennedy and the High School graduated its first class in 1930.

On the opposite page is an early photo of Gallup, New Mexico, one of a number of towns that sprang up along the route of the old Atlantic and Pacific Railroad (now the Santa Fe R.R.). Prior to 1880, the site was occupied by a saloon and general store called the Blue Goose and served as a stopping place for the Westward Overland Stage. A paymaster for the railroad, David L. Gallup, established his office here during the construction period and the town received its name by the workers who would speak of "going to Gallup to get paid". It is now a major trading center for both Navajos and Zunis.

A gathering of Navajos, government officials and clergymen at St. Michaels in the early 1900's. Sitting on the edge of the bench in center foreground is Chee Dodge. The Franciscan mission was established in 1898 by Fr. Juvenal Schnorbus and Fr. Anslem Weber. The Sisters of the Blessed Sacrament opened an elementary school in 1902 and the high school in 1946. In the years before the formation of the Tribal Council the Franciscans played a valuable role in lending legal assistance and financial support to the Navajos in their efforts to settle land disputes.

A representative form of Tribal government had its beginnings in 1921 when a general council was convened at the San Juan Agency to consider and approve the leasing of land for the development of oil and gas wells. Two years later a council was elected which consisted of two delegates from each of the six Agencies plus a Chairman. The Council met annually, primarily to consider land leases, until it was reorganized in 1936.

The Tribal Council meeting in 1934 was held in Crownpoint, headquarters for the Eastern Navajo Agency. Foremost on the agenda was consideration of the Wheeler-Howard Act (the Indian Reorganization Act). After considerable debate it was then put to a general vote of the people and rejected by a narrow margin. The two photos at left show some of the crowd who turned out for the Council meeting, which was held rather informally out-of-doors.

The Tribal Council as it existed in 1934. In the dark suit is James Stewart, then Head of the Branch of Realty, Washington Office talking to Thomas Dodge, Council Chairman, and Jacob Morgan. To the left of Dodge are Frank Cadman, Billy Becenti, Lee Bradley, and Chic Sandoval. To the right of Stewart (front row) are Allen Neshaki, George Bancroft, Fred Nelson, Marcus Kanuho, and Henry Taliman, all members of the 12-man Tribal Council.

For centuries, this natural window, known as Tseghahodzani, (Perforated Rock) was a sacred place in Navajo Ceremonialism, especially in the Water Way Ceremony. In 1935, when the structure of Navajo administration was reorganized and the various agencies consolidated into one, John Collier, Commissioner of Indian Affairs, selected this site for the Navajo Central Agency. Buildings of russet-colored sandstone, quarried in the vicinity, were constructed for use by the Bureau of Indian Affairs, the Navajo Tribe, and Public Health Service (pictured below).

Against a backdrop of scenic red sandstone cliffs and the majestic window itself, the administrative capitol of the vast Navajo Reservation has continued to grow in both size and importance. It is the seat of the 74-member Navajo Tribal Council, whose Chamber can be seen at lower left. Laid out along the curved streets are office buildings for the Bureau of Indian Affairs, the Tribal Divisions of Administration, Resources, and Public Services, the Public Health Service and United States Post Office, as well as a restaurant, motel, bank, and employee's homes.

The father-son team that was very influential in the development of the Tribal government. At left Henry Chee Dodge (1860-1946) was a member of the Business Council of 1922. When the 12-man Tribal Council was established in 1923, he was chosen as Chairman and served until 1928. He again served as Chairman from 1942-1946. His son, Thomas Dodge (right) served as Chairman from 1932-1936.

In 1937, a Constitutional Assembly was convened for the purpose of again reorganizing the Tribal Council. The Assembly was attended by nearly 250 Navajo headman who selected Henry Taliman as Chairman. Taliman is shown at right with John Collier, Commissioner of Indian Affairs at the time of the Constitutional Assembly and under whose administration the controversial stock reduction program was initiated. The Secretary of the Interior did not approve the constitution as drafted, but did agree to a set of regulations which included election procedures, a definition of organization of the governing body, a statement of its powers and a description of its mode of operation.

In the general election of 1938, an expanded 74-member council was elected with Jacob Morgan as Chairman. Four years later, in 1942, the Chairmanship went to Chee Dodge, with Sam Ahkeah as Vice-Chairman. During these war years, the Navajo Tribe faced very trying times, with construction, road improvements and expansion of utilities brought almost to a standstill. Shown below is James Stewart, Agency Superintendent, addressing the Tribal Council. Seated behind him is (l to r) Chee Dodge, Julius Krug (Sec. of Interior), and Ernest McFarland (Arizona Senator).

In the campaign of 1945 the two top officials switched places on the ballot, with Sam Ahkeah running for Chairman and Chee Dodge for Vice-Chairman. However, in January, 1946, Chee Dodge died before taking office and the position was filled by Zhealy Tso. In the election of 1950, the use of pictorial paper ballots was substituted for colored ribbons and the institution of voter registration was introduced. Sam Ahkeah was again victorious and took his oath of office from Judge Hatch on March 30, 1951 (shown at left).

After World War II, national attention was directed to the deplorable conditions existing on the Navajo and Hopi Reservations. In 1948 a report was compiled under a directive from J. A. Krug, Secretary of the Interior. It pointed out that in the 25,000 square miles of reservation lands there were only 466 hospital beds, 95 miles of paved roads, school facilities for only 7,500 students, 3 restaurants, and 763 telephones. Less than 800 Navajos had full time jobs, while 7,841 persons were on welfare. Through the concerted efforts of both the Bureau of Indian Affairs and the Navajo Tribe, a long range, three-purpose program was developed. This program aspired to (1) enable the Navajo people to attain economic self-sufficiency through their own efforts; (2) assist them in becoming healthy and educated citizens, capable of enjoying the full benefits of

our society; and (3) carry out the legal and moral obligations of the Federal Government to the Navajo Tribe. On April 19, 1950, Congress approved the Navajo-Hopi Long Range Rehabilitation Act and appropriated ninety million dollars to be used over a ten year period. Many of the projects outlined by this Act were initiated by the Council shown in the above picture taken in 1951. The second row, from left to right includes Paul Jones, interpreter, Advisory Committee members George Hubbard, Adolph Maloney, Frank Bradley, Clifford Beck, Leo Parker, Billy Becenti, Sam Ahkeah (Chairman), John Claw (Vice-Chairman), Howard Gorman, Yellowman, and Grey Valentine. Standing behind Parker is Allan Harper, Area Director. Behind Becenti is John Todea, Secretary-Treasurer for the Tribal Council.

In August, 1952, the World War II hero and future President of the United States, Dwight Eisenhower, visited the Inter-tribal Indian Ceremonial at Gallup, New Mexico. Hosting "Ike" are Dan Thornton, Governor of Colorado, Ed Mechem, Governor of New Mexico, Sam Ahkeah, Chairman of the Navajo Tribal Council, and Howard Pyle, Governor of Arizona.

In the Tribal elections of 1954, Sam Ahkeah, running for a third term, was opposed, and defeated, by Paul Jones and Scott Preston. This was the first tribal election conducted solely by the Tribe itself, as all previous elections had been supervised by the Bureau of Indian Affairs. Major problems facing the new council were focused on improving health and education facilities, settlement of the Navajo-Hopi Boundary dispute and the development of a Tribally-operated police force. Some of the members of that Council included (left to right, front row) Hoska Cronemeyer, Roger Davis, Dillon Platero and John Perry.

Land useage and ownership in areas bordering the reservation became critical problems in the 1950's. One such situation regarded the long-time Navajo use and occupancy of certain portions of San Juan County, Utah. Chairman Paul Jones assists (above) in taking the testimony of Mr. Split Rock (center) and Francis Warren, a victim of an alleged beating by a member of the San Juan County Sheriff's department during removal of Navajo stock from the contested area.

Three candidates entered the 1962 Tribal elections. Running for Chairman were the incumbent, Paul Jones, Samuel Billison, and Raymond Nakai. In the hotly-contested race, Nakai emerged the winner and was inaugurated on April 13, 1963 (shown above). Four years later, in 1966, Nakai was elected for a second term, and stated in his inaugural speech, "The accomplishments to which we point to with pride has awakened in all of us a sense of new hope and confidence, and a will to succeed in that which has been started and the will to undertake new commitments."

Under the Nakai administration, several new industries have established themselves on the Reservation, the Office of Navajo Economic Opportunity was organized, and an accelerated highway construction program was developed. National attention has been focused on the Navajos' successful attempts to diligently solve their own socio-economic problems. This was exemplified recently by the visit paid to Navajoland by the Vice-President of the United States. At a banquet in his honor were, seated from left to right, Nelson Damon, Vice-Chairman, Mrs. Raymond Nakai, Hubert Humphrey, Vice-President, Raymond Nakai, Chairman, and Sam Goddard, former governor of Arizona.

THE RESOLUTION

WHEREAS, The Navajo Tribal Council and the fifty thousand people we represent, cannot fail to recognize the crisis now facing the world in the threat of foreign invasion and the destruction of the great liberties and benefits which we enjoy on our Reservation, and

WHEREAS, there exists no purer concentration of Americanism than among the First Americans, and

WHEREAS, it has become common practice to attempt national destruction through the sowing of seeds of treachery among minority groups such as ours, and

WHEREAS, we may expect such activity among our people,

THEREFORE, we hereby serve notice that any un-American movement among our people will be resented and dealt with severely, and

NOW, THEREFORE, we resolve that the Navajo

With the Japanese attack on Pearl Harbor, the United States plunged into World War II, and on December 9, 1941, issued a Call To Arms. In the finest traditions of a proud warrior society, Navajos, along with Indians from throughout the country, flocked to the recruiting stations, such as the one pictured at right being manned by John McPhee (seated) and Frank Walker (second from left). In they came, old-timers with muskets, former cavalry scouts, and young men with such a spontaneous display of loyalty and patriotism that, by the time the war was over, there were more enlistments among the Indians, in proportion to their numbers, than any other racial group in the country. Navajos were among the New Mexico National Guard troops that surrendered at Bataan, and were also with the 45th Division which invaded Italy. Navajos fought in every theatre of the war - from the Aleutian Islands to North Africa, from the beaches of Normandy to the jungles of the South Pacific — an impressive record to be truly proud of.

Indians stand ready as they did in 1918, to aid and defend our Government and its institutions against all subversive and armed conflict and pledge our loyalty to the system which recognizes minority rights and a way of life that has placed us among the greatest people of our race.

Passed by unanimous vote of the Navajo Tribal Council at Window Rock, Arizona, this 3rd day of June, Nineteen Hundred and Forty.

    (Signed) J. C. Morgan, Chairman.
    (Signed) Howard Gorman, Vice-Chairman.

Early in the war, the Military recognized the value of the Navajo language as a means of sending messages, rather than using codes. A group of 29 young Navajos were recruited by the Marine Corps from the boarding schools at Ft. Defiance, Ft. Wingate, and Shiprock and given special training at San Diego as signalmen and translators. This group, organized as the 382nd Platoon, U. S. Marine Corps, was such a success in the South Pacific, that recruiting officers traveled throughout the reservation, looking for educated young Navajos who were physically fit for the rugged life of a combat communications specialist. Before the war ended, the Marine Corps enrolled 375 Navajo code-talkers, who saw action in Africa, Sicily, Italy and the South Pacific.

Pictured above (May, 1942), with their three non-commissioned officers, are the first Navajo code-talkers at their training camp near San Diego, California. Front row (left to right): Frank Pete, Corporal L. P. Kohl, Sgt. L. J. Stephenson, Corporal R. J. Hays, and Willsie Bitsie. Second row: Chester Nez, Eugene Crawford, John Brown, Cosey Brown, Johnnie Benallie, William Yazzie, Benjamin Cleveland, and Nelson Thompson. Third row: Lloyd Oliver, Charlie Begay, William Mc-Cabe, Oscar Ilthma, David Curley, Lowell Damon, Balmer Slowtalker, Alfred Leonard, and Dale June. Top row: James Dixon, Roy Begay, James Manuelito, Harry Tsosie, George Dennison, Carl Gorman, Samuel Begay, John Chee, Jack Nez, and John Willie.

Navajos pitched in on the home front, too. Hundreds went to work in the fields and orchards throughout California and Oregon, and men whose lack of English disqualified them from military service, worked on the railroads. The Army built two large ordnance depots for the manufacture of bombs and grenades near the reservation and employed Navajos both for the construction of the plants and as assembly-line workers. One depot was built on the grounds of old Ft. Wingate, and the other just west of Flagstaff, Arizona. The pictures at left, taken at Ft. Wingate in the early 1940's show (top) a Navajo still in traditional dress, operating a primer press for ammunition, and (bottom) three Navajos loading casings containing 105 MM Howitzer shells into a railroad car for shipment to the West Coast.

Ever since the return from Ft. Sumner, the federal government was faced with the problem of effective communication and contact between itself and the Navajo people. In an effort to resolve this problem, John Hunter, Superintendent of the Leupp Agency, in 1927, began the development of local community organizations which came to be known as Chapters. An early picture of one such meeting is shown at right. These meetings were designed to bring the Navajo people together at a local level where representatives of the Tribe, B.I.A. and Public Health Service could more effectively explain and gather support for their programs and objectives.

For a while after its inception, the Chapter movement spread rapidly and became a popular forum for local politics. However, during the controversial period of stock reduction and range control (between 1932 and 1950) this movement lost its popularity and was temporarily halted. In 1950 the program was revived and since that date has steadily expanded and gained strength, mainly because its form of organization is more in keeping with traditional Navajo social patterns. In 1956, when Tribal income increased sharply as a result of new oil leases, an appropriation was authorized and plans developed for expansion of the Chapter system on a Reservation-wide basis. Under terms of Council resolution CM-46-57, adopted in May, 1958, an appropriation of $2,500,000 over a 5-year period was authorized for the construction, repair and maintenance of Chapter houses. The program was placed under the direction of the Public Services Division, which at that time recognized 85 Chapter organizations. Since then, fifteen new Chapters have been certified, the latest being Rough Rock, thus increasing the number to 100. The goal is to provide each Chapter with a modern community house which will serve as a local government building as well as providing facilities for educational, social, and recreational programs for the surrounding area.

77

From time immemorial the People have been farmers, making their livelihood from the riches of the soil. Centuries ago, their neighbors, the Pueblo Indians referred to them as "Nabahoe" or "Cultivator of the fields" and it has been an apt description ever since. Dry farming is still practiced throughout Navajoland with families annually gathering together to clear the land; then plant, cultivate and harvest their crops. Many of the foods grown today are those that were originally domesticated and developed by the American Indian - corn, beans, potatoes, and a wide variety of squashes, melons and pumpkins. Crops are raised primarily for home consumption.

As early as 1880, an effort was made to develop water resources to meet agricultural and livestock needs. Over the years, about 67 irrigation projects have been completed, ranging in size from a few acres to several thousand. At present, there are over 35,000 acres of irrigated land being utilized, primarily along the San Juan river in New Mexico (shown below), and in the Ganado, Many Farms and Red Lake areas in Arizona. This will eventually be supplemented by an additional 110,000 acres which will be developed in the near future under the Navajo-San Juan Project. A successful Farm Training Program is being jointly sponsored by both the Navajo Tribe and the Bureau of Indian Affairs.

Since the middle of the 18th century, livestock raising has also been an important factor in the economy of the Navajo Tribe. A severe blow was dealt this economy in the 1860's when the U. S. Army conducted a "scorched earth policy" during the Navajo campaign and destroyed thousands of sheep, cattle and horses. Blizzards and severe weather, too, have taken their toll of Navajo livestock. To alleviate the problem, in several serious instances, the Federal Government in 1956 (shown at left) and again in 1967 made grain and hay available for livestock stranded in the heavy snows,

A necessary, but very traumatic episode occured in the 1930's when the government instituted the Stock Reduction Program. Because of continued and widespread overgrazing, the rangelands and watersheds were fast deteriorating. The program left many of the smaller livestock owners completely improvished but through the years, the gradual improvement of the land and deversity of income has somewhat bettered conditions. Greatly improved methods of raising and maintaining livestock have been successfully introduced through the efforts of the Tribe, Bureau of Indian Affairs, Agricultural Extension Service, Conservation Program and 4-H Clubs.

Returning servicemen, at the end of World War II, brought back to the Reservation an awareness and new understanding of the importance of education in their lives and the lives of their children. Cultural isolationism was now a thing of the past.

In 1946, the Tribe sent a delegation to Washington to seek solutions to the problems of providing more and better equipped schools for thousands of educationally deprived Navajo youngsters. Several programs developed to partially satisfy the growing Navajo demand for better education.

An accelerated building program, meant only as a stop-gap measure, produced quonset hut (top) and trailer day schools throughout the more remote areas. Existing schools were crammed to capacity (above), and a special Five Year Program for teen-age Navajos was initiated.

The phenomenal growth of the Navajo Tribe since the end of World War II has put primary emphasis on school construction and expanding existing facilities. In 1945 the Navajo population numbered 61,000 of whom more than 20,000 were of school age; but less than 6,000 were enrolled.

By 1958 the number of school age children had increased to 30,000, and in 1967 had further increased to 45,000. Through accelerated programs and the expenditure of many millions of dollars, public, parochial, and government schools can now accommodate 95% of the school age children.

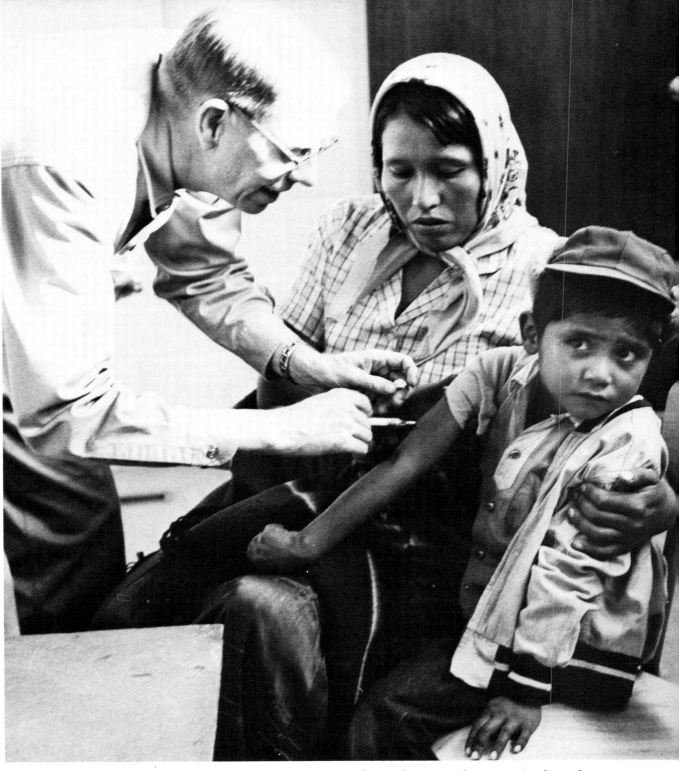

The health status of the Navajos too, gained the attention of the Federal government during the late 1940's. The diseases which particularly afflicted the Navajo people were tuberculosis, pneumonia, and diarrheal diseases. Most of these exacted a heavy toll of Navajo lives, especially those of infants and small children. In 1952, the Navajo health level lagged almost two generations behind that of the general population. A special health program was incorporated into the Long-Range Rehabilitation Act of 1950 which sought to attack the problem on four fronts: (1) to remodel, expand or replace hospital facilities with emphasis on the care of tubercular patients, (2) to establish a system of field stations, or clinics, (3) to develop itinerant medical and dental services, and (4) to provide an adequate public health program. In an effort to consolidate the various health and medical programs throughout the United States, Congress enacted Public Law 568 which went into effect July 1, 1955. This Law transferred full responsibility for the Indian health program from the BIA Branch of Health, to the Public Health Service in the Department of Health, Education and Welfare.

Six field general hospitals as well as numerous clinics and several mission hospitals presently serve the Navajo. The field hospitals are located at Ft. Defiance (159 beds), Crownpoint (65 beds), Winslow (53 beds), Shiprock (75 beds), Gallup (200 beds), and Tuba City (75 beds) shown above. The new facilities at Tuba City were completed in 1954, at Shiprock in 1960, and at Gallup in 1961.

With expanded facilities and staffs the Public Health Service has embarked on new activities to extend needed services—such as maternal and child health, nutrition, sanitation, and health education. By providing these preventive services at the home level, the program decreases the number of advanced infectious diseases seen at the hospital. Through the joint efforts of the Navajo Tribe and PHS, Health Education aides conduct family-level courses on such subjects as diarrhea control, fly control, immunizations, dry skim milk, and trachoma.

85

For many years, the daughter of Chee Dodge, Mrs. Annie Wauneka, has concerned herself with the problems of disease, child sickness, and home sanitation on the Navajo reservation. She has been one of only a few women to be elected to the Navajo Tribal Council and served for several years as chairwoman of the Health Committee. In recognition of her services, she was presented the Medal of Freedom at White House ceremonies on December 6, 1963, (above) the only Navajo ever to receive this high honor. The citation read,

"The President of the United States of America awards this Presidential Medal of Freedom to Annie Dodge Wauneka, first woman elected to the Navajo Tribal Council, by her long crusade for improved health programs, she helped dramatically to lessen the menace of disease among her people and to improve their way of life. (signed) Lyndon B. Johnson." Two years later the Columbia Broadcasting System filmed a documentary on Mrs. Wauneka's activities. It was presented on the TV series "20th Century."

The acquirement of sufficient water has always been a matter of top priority throughout Navajoland. Prior to 1930, water development had proceeded slowly, with only 51 reservoirs, 321 springs, 161 dug wells, 77 drilled wells, and 23 artesian wells being developed by that time (photo above). A range water survey made in 1931 resulted in an initial water development program carried on between 1933 and 1936. During this period, 730 reservoirs, 158 drilled wells, 332 springs and 273 dug wells were completed. The Tribe made its first appropriation for water development purposes in fiscal year 1952, and had completely assumed the responsibilities of this function from the Federal government by 1960. During the decade of the 1950's, through the joint efforts of both the Tribe and the Bureau of Indian Affairs, 490 drilled wells alone were completed throughout Navajoland. To date, over eight million dollars of both Tribal and Federal funds have been expended on water development.

Resource development has taken great strides within the past two decades, primarily in the fields of oil and gas, coal, electricity, and rare metals. In 1950, there were 51 oil wells on the Reservation producing an annual yield of 133,173 barrels (at right). Today, nearly a thousand wells produce two hundred times that amount. Since 1935, more than $140,000,000, in bonuses, leases and royalties have been realized by the Navajo Tribe, of which nearly 10% has been received since 1957. The need both locally and throughout the Southwest, for more electrical power has prompted the development of two coal fields to supply fuel for newly constructed generating plants.

The Four-Corners power plant near Shiprock is utilizing a nearby coal deposit (below) covering more than 25,000 acres. Power from this plant is transmitted 300 miles to Phoenix over a 340,000 volt line shown under construction on the opposite page.

One of the first pieces of equipment brought in by the newly established railroad in 1880 was a portable sawmill. It was set up in the Fluted Rock area and used to cut lumber for agency, school, and mission construction purposes. The logs were skidded to the mill by ox-team; an operation that continued until 1907. In that year, a new mill was built in the Toadlena area to provide lumber for construction of the Shiprock Agency. This mill burned in 1935, and all salvageable equipment was transferred to a new site 15 miles northwest of Ft. Defiance. This plant became known simply as Sawmill, Arizona, and in 1936 came under the jurisdiction of the Navajo Agency Forester. At right, Marion Brown operates the 8-foot band saw.

90

Construction of the facilities at Sawmill, Arizona, began in 1935, but the operation was only intermittent and inadequately financed. In 1939, the Tribe borrowed $50,000 to rebuild the plant and in the following year an additional sum of $165,000 for expansion purposes. This debt was paid off in 1944 when the mill achieved self-supporting status as an enterprise of the Navajo Tribe. The mill (left), employed approximately 300 workers and continued operating at a profit until it was shut down in May. 1963.

Approximately 5% of Navajoland, or 760,800 acres, is covered with a fine stand of coniferous timber, primarily ponderosa pine. However, less than two- thirds of this area is accessible and can therefore be used for commercial purposes. The Tribe's merchantable timber lies mainly on the 458,457 acre area comprising the Defiance and Chuska-Tsaile units and amounts to over 2,087,000,000 board feet. In recent years, expanded logging operations provide employment for nearly 200 Navajos, and have created a net-work of roads in the previously inaccessible mountain regions. The sustained yield harvest presently amounts to 43,000,000 board feet, but in 1977 this will be reduced to 33,000,000.

In 1958, the Navajo Tribal Council appropriated $7,500,000 for construction of a new, modern sawmill and created the Navajo Forest Products Industries to manage the expanded operation. By September, 1962, the basic construction was completed and the sawmill put into operation (pictured at left). Today, Navajo Pine is marketed throughout the Southwest and as far east as Michigan, Ohio and Indiana. By-products produced include pulp chips which are shipped to a paper plant at Snowflake, Arizona; graded bark chips used in agricultural and landscaping purposes; and the manufacture of pre-fab homes.

93

During the decade of the 1950's, under the provisions of the Long Range Rehabilitation Act, many construction projects were undertaken in order to bolster the Navajo economy. These projects were primarily involved in school, road and hospital construction and were designed to offer on-the-job training to Navajo workmen. This program not only alleviated, to some extent, the unemployment situation on the Reservation, but gave many Navajos the training and skills necessary to acquire work on projects off the Reservation through the Relocation Program.

Throughout the width and breadth of Navajoland one can feel and see the vitality of a people bent on bettering their lives. Utilizing age-old talents of stone masonry and combining old methods with new, Navajos are working on projects ranging from Chapter Houses and Community Centers to roadside rest stops and school bus shelters. New facilities have been constructed at nearly all the Chapters and modern Civic Centers are now located at Window Rock, Chinle, Shiprock and Tuba City. Branch offices for the Arts and Crafts Guild as well as other Tribal and Government agencies have recently been constructed within the communities of Chinle, Crownpoint, Kayenta, Ft. Defiance, Shiprock and Tuba City.

As an adjunct to the industrial development of Navajoland, proper and adequate facilities had to be constructed first. Housing had top priority and several projects were developed simultaneously beginning in the early 1960's. Assisted by government financing, a 72-unit project was initiated at Window Rock in 1962, followed shortly by similar projects at Navajo, New Mexico, and near Shiprock. Recently, over 500 low-rent units have been made available at several of the major communities throughout Navajoland.

The Depression and Stock Reduction program of the 1930's made it only too evident that the Navajo people would have to diversify their economy if they were to survive. Accordingly, the Tribe adopted a policy of encouraging and enticing industries to relocate on or near the Navajo Reservation. Until recently, lack of housing, utilities and roads hampered this development. Three major electronics firms are presently the major wage providers; Fairchild (above) in Shiprock, General Dynamics in Ft. Defiance, and EPI Vostrun at Page, Arizona.

Tribal construction has also included such facilities as motels and restaurants to accommodate the growing number of visitors to Navajoland. The Tribe, by this time, was beginning to actively encourage tourism.

One of the major attractions for visitor and Navajo alike were, and still are, the annual Tribal Fairs held every autumn in Window Rock (above) and Shiprock. The first Fair was initiated at Shiprock in 1909 by Superintendent William Shelton but did not become an annual event until 1923.

The fairgrounds near Window Rock were originally laid out in 1937, but the Fair was not held during the War years or the years immediately following. Revived in 1947, the Fair has grown from its rustic beginnings (shown above) to an event that now attracts over 70,000 spectators.

With the completion of the Civic Center in 1958, the Fair took on the aspects of a modern exposition, but still retains much of it colorful past. The Fair opens each year with a free barbecue attended by thousands of people, which is followed by four days of rodeos, horse racing, Indian dances, 4-H competitions, Miss Navajo contests, carnival rides and parades. Several exhibit halls proudly display a wide variety of agricultural produce, livestock, arts & crafts, home arts, and exhibits (above) presented by schools, missions, businesses, Tribal, B.I.A. & Public Health agencies.

The Economic Opportunity Act of 1964 afforded the Navajo Tribe an excellent chance to expand its plans and administer its own programs in alleviating poverty and illiteracy. In the fall of 1964, the Tribal Advisory Committee established the Office of Navajo Economic Opportunity and by April, 1965, the first federal grant of funds to ONEO was approved by the Washington office of OEO. Under the Executive Directorship of Peter McDonald, the program has expanded rapidly within the past few years. One of the best-known programs to have come into existance under ONEO is the Child Development, or Pre-School program. Pre-school preparation has been a long-recognized need as the transition from home environment to school environment is a difficult experience for most Navajo children, especially those who come from homes where English is not spoken. The Pre-School program (above) gives the child a head start in making these necessary adjustments.

The primary purpose of many of the programs of the Office of Navajo Economic Opportunity has been to improve the living conditions throughout Navajoland. The sewing class shown above is typical of the many self-improvement projects being undertaken and financed by ONEO. Other successful programs designed and sponsored by the Office of Navajo Economic Opportunity, besides the Child Development, are local Community Development, Home Improvement Training, Navajo Culture Center, Small Business Development Center, Neighborhood Youth Corps, Migrant and Agriculture Placement, Alcoholism Treatment, Legal Aid, (Dinebiina Nahiilna Be Agaditahe Inc.), Recreation and Arts & Crafts Training, and VISTA (Volunteers In Service To America).

Traditionally, Navajo society maintained order without the formality of an established court and police system. The religious system of taboos and informal laws placed great value on the maintenance of a harmonious relationship between man and his environment. However, as the many complex facets of Anglo society became more and more absorbed into Navajo culture, it became necessary to adopt a unified code of law and an effective system of enforcement and control.

For several decades following the return from Ft. Sumner, cavalry troops were used to maintain law and order while the Agent acted in the capacity of judge and jury. This responsibility was gradually assumed by the Bureau of Indian Affairs who used the police primarily to bring Navajo children to school and to apprehend truants. During the 1930's Courts of Indian Offenses were established, manned by six Navajo judges appointed to office by the Commissioner of Indian Affairs with the confirmation of the Tribal Council. During the period 1951-1959 the judges were elected to office by popular vote in Tribal elections. Since 1959, the judges, including the Chief Justice, are appointed on a lifetime basis. These courts hear all cases stemming from civil and criminal disputes with the exception of the eleven major crimes. This system has the advantage of providing the defendant the opportunity of having his case heard by a jury of his peers, whereby both tribal customs and the legal code are taken into consideration.

The Navajo Mounted Police were
established in 1934 and reorganized as
the Navajo Patrol in 1936 (shown above).
This subsequently became known as the
Branch of Law and Order, which, in 1959,
was transferred to Tribal jurisdiction
and reorganized as the Navajo Police
Department. At left, Captain Adakai
converses with one of his patrolmen in
front of the new Judicial-Police
headquarters at Window Rock.

105

The Navajo Council, during the 1950's, became more and more aware of the economic advantages of a program aimed at promoting tourism, as well as the need to control and minimize vandalism in the many archaeological sites throughout Navajoland. In order to better confront this two-fold problem, the Tribal Council, in 1957, established the Navajo Tribal Parks Commission and appointed Sam Day III as its chairman. Under the guidance and supervision of this Commission, the Department of Parks and Recreation was organized and a force of Navajo Rangers established. Several areas of Reservation land, because of their outstanding scenic or historical significance, were subsequently withdrawn as Navajo Tribal Parks. The first of these, established in 1960, was Monument Valley where a Visitor Center (shown at right) and scenic loop drive are maintained by Navajo Rangers. Presently, there are seven Tribal Parks and seven National Monuments and Historic Sites within Navajoland with an annual aggregate visitation of well over a million people, thus making Tourism one of the major sources of income throughout the Navajo country.

The Navajo Tribal Museum, established in August, 1961, is dedicated to the preservation and presentation of the cultural heritage of the Navajo people and the natural sciences of the Navajo country. It is administered as a section within the Department of Parks and Recreation. The Museum's collections are among the finest and most complete that can be found in any Museum of comparable size and contain thousands of articles of Navajo manufacture as well as artifacts from other Southwest Indian tribes and pre-historic cultures. The exhibits are primarily related to the history, religion, and crafts of the Navajo, but also include displays on the geology, paleontology, botany, and the Anasazi culture as well. In 1962, a small zoo was added to give a broader interpretive scope to the biological exhibits. Research facilities at the Museum include a very comprehensive library, photo collection, and herbarium. During the past several years, several salvage archaeological surveys and excavations have been completed. The museum is also involved in a very diverse educational program. A series of books is published periodically as well as numerous pamphlets and brochures. Staff members present programs and lectures to civic organizations and school groups throughout the entire Southwest. Well over 8,000 Navajo school children visit the Museum and zoo annually. The most important role of the Museum, however, is to afford the Navajo people with a link to their past and their traditions. Thus, each and every Navajo has the opportunity to renew his faith in himself and to build a sense of pride and identity with his cultural heritage.

"The Century of Progress which we commemorate
has not been an easy one hundred years. It was
initiated by the tragic and heartbreaking 'long march'
from Ft. Sumner. It marked a struggle of a proud
people, accustomed to roam unfettered over the vast
expanses of this great western United States. It
reflects the slow, but steady progress of our people to
this very moment. However difficult has been our
struggle, never was the faith of the Navajo people the
least bit diminished in their ultimate place in
society. Never did the Navajo despair. Always, he
sought and fought for a better way of life.
All in all, this past one hundred years does reflect
great progress on the part of our people. But we are
at the very beginning of our true development.
I shall not be here when the second centennial of
the Navajo Nation is commemorated, but let me here
give the next one hundred years a name. As the first
has been called a Century of Progress, let the
second be called a Century of Achievement.
We are, indeed, on the threshold of great
achievements for our people in the fields of
education, industrial development, and economic
well-being. The next decades will witness giant
steps forward in these areas.
Yes, we are on a 'long march' again — a march
forward and upward — a march toward achievement
for all that is good for our people.
It shall require the best in all of us to reach our goal
for our sights are high, and we will not be content
with mere modest achievements.
Let us resolve to make this next one hundred years
a great century for our people, so that our children's
children, in the year 2068, can announce with pride
— 'This past one hundred years has been, indeed,
a century of Great Achievement'."

RAYMOND NAKAI
Speech delivered at Opening of the Centennial Year

ACKNOWLEDGMENTS

I wish to express my appreciation, and
give proper credit and recognition to the
following institutions for use of the
photographs appearing in this book:
Bureau of American Ethnology,
Smithsonian Institute; Signal Corps,
National Archives; Ben Wittick
Collection, New Mexico State Museum;
Simeon Schwemberger Collection, St.
Michaels Mission; Tom Mullarky
Collection, Mullarky Photo Shop; Jack
Snow Collection, Bureau of Indian
Affairs; and the Navajo Tribal
Photograph Collection. A few of
the photographs are my own.
Statistical information has been extracted
from various sources, including
Navajo Tribal records and the Navajo
Yearbook VIII, by Robert Young.
The book was designed by Robert
Jacobson, Northern Arizona University.

M.A.L.